Original title:
Starlit Snowfall

Copyright © 2024 Swan Charm
All rights reserved.

Author: Liina Liblikas
ISBN HARDBACK: 978-9908-52-059-9
ISBN PAPERBACK: 978-9908-52-060-5
ISBN EBOOK: 978-9908-52-061-2

Woven Lights in the Cold Embrace

In the hush of winter's breath,
Stars flicker in the vast expanse,
A tapestry of dreams entwined,
Woven lights in a mystic dance.

Silvery glitter on frozen streams,
Moon whispers softly on icy ground,
Echoes of warmth wrapped in silence,
Where hope in the dark is found.

Cold air sparkles, a shimmering sight,
Each flake a whisper from above,
A gentle reminder of the night,
Crafted with care, a lesson of love.

Stillness settles like a soft lullaby,
Embracing the world in pure delight,
In winter's arms, we find our sigh,
Woven lights bring solace to the night.

A Spell of White Beneath the Firmament

A blanket of snow covers the earth,
Whispers of magic in silence unfurl,
Beneath the firmament, a timeless birth,
A spell of white over all, a pearl.

Gentle flakes dance on the wind,
Caressing the trees with delicate grace,
Nature's canvas, where dreams rescind,
A peaceful wonder, a tranquil place.

Footprints linger in powdered trails,
Led by the heart to where wishes reside,
In the hush, a promise prevails,
A quiet moment where hopes collide.

Stars twinkle down from a velvet sky,
Illuminating paths we dare to roam,
In the spell of white, we learn to fly,
Finding in winter, a place called home.

When Snow meets the Veil of Night

When snow meets the veil of night,
Soft whispers echo in chilly air,
A canvas stretched in purest white,
Dreams awaken, free from care.

Moonlight reflects on crystalline ground,
Painting shadows, a mystic scene,
In the stillness, lost dreams are found,
Where silence reigns, pure and serene.

Branches bow with a heavy load,
Crystals glisten in the moon's soft gaze,
In the night, the secrets encode,
Filling hearts with a soft, warm blaze.

Time stands still in this frozen world,
Promises linger in frosty air,
As night unfurls its magic swirled,
Painting beauty, beyond compare.

Chilling Reflections of Twilight Glory

In twilight's embrace, the day takes flight,
Chilling reflections of a world aglow,
Colors blend as darkness ignites,
In the stillness, the whispers flow.

Frosted air carries silent tales,
Softly echoing in twilight's dome,
An artist's brush where twilight prevails,
Crafting visions of warmth from cold.

In every shadow, mysteries play,
A dance of light on the frosty ground,
As day sinks low, night finds its way,
In chilling reflections, magic is found.

Stars emerge, twinkling bright,
A symphony born from the fading day,
In the heart of night, pure and right,
Twilight's glory, forever to stay.

A Dazzle of Light on Crisp White

Morning sun climbs high,
Dancing on the fresh snow,
Whispers of soft light,
A bright and pure glow.

Footsteps leave a trace,
In this world of magic,
Every flake a gem,
In beauty's sturdy guise.

Shadows play and twirl,
Nature's sparkling adorn
A tapestry unfurls,
In glittering adornment.

The air sparkles bright,
With each breath that we take,
A dazzle of delight,
In this serene landscape.

Winter's kiss is sweet,
A fleeting, cold embrace,
On the canvas white,
Life finds its quiet grace.

Fragments of Frost in Silver Gleam

Early morn reveals,
Branches wrapped in crystal,
Nature's sharp appeal,
In a world so tranquil.

Each frost-kissed surface,
Casts a radiant glow,
Fragments of pure lace,
In winter's gentle flow.

The earth holds its breath,
As beauty's veil descends,
In fragile silence,
Time seems to suspend.

A silver touch graces,
Every thing it can find,
In frozen embraces,
Nature's calm unwind.

An art made of frost,
In whispers from the sky,
In moments embossed,
Where the heart learns to sigh.

The Magic of Ice Under Starlit Veils

Beneath the vast sky,
Stars shimmer like diamonds,
On frozen rivers,
Nature's mystic bands.

Veils of shimmering light,
Enchant the silent night,
Every crystal reflects,
Memories held so tight.

The moon casts its spell,
On the sparkling expanse,
Drawing dreams that dwell,
In a soft, sacred dance.

Footprints on the ice,
Tell stories of the past,
Echoes of a voice,
Whispering, ever vast.

In the cold embrace,
Magic holds the night tight,
Wrapped in pure grace,
Under the starry flight.

Chasing Shadows on the Snow

Morning breaks anew,
As shadows start to play,
In the crisp, bright dew,
Chasing light all day.

Footprints lead the way,
In patterns soft and bold,
While shadows sway,
In stories yet untold.

The sun casts long lines,
Drawing the day's wide breath,
Every path defines,
A dance of life or death.

Chasing what remains,
In a world dressed in white,
Where joy sometimes gains,
In the fleeting light.

Winter's fleeting grace,
Moments lost in the flow,
Each step we embrace,
In shadows on the snow.

Ethereal Dance of Ice and Light

In twilight's glow, the ice does gleam,
A ballet spun from winter's dream.
It sways with grace in chilly air,
A spectacle both bright and rare.

Each crystal twirls, a fleeting spark,
Reflecting hues from light's soft arc.
They whisper secrets, soft and low,
As night descends on white below.

Underneath the silver sky,
The frozen dance won't say goodbye.
It lingers on, a fleeting chance,
Entwined, we watch the ice's dance.

With every turn, the night is spun,
The world transformed, the day is done.
In stillness deep, this art takes flight,
An ethereal dance of ice and light.

Frost-Kissed Reveries at Twilight

As day retreats, the frost arrives,
In softest whispers, nature strives.
Each blade adorned with jewel bright,
A tapestry of cold delight.

The breezes hum a gentle tune,
Beneath the watchful, glimmering moon.
With every breath, the world exhales,
In dreams of winter, wonder prevails.

The golden glow of sun's last rays,
Caresses frost in tender plays.
The twilight wraps the earth so tight,
In frost-kissed reveries, pure and light.

In cozy corners, shadows loom,
While nature dons her silver bloom.
And gentle dreams of night's embrace,
Inviting peace in this bright space.

Celestial Drift of Shimmering White

Gentle flakes fall from the sky,
A snowy drift that catches eye.
Each flake a star, so soft, so bright,
In celestial dance, a wondrous sight.

They blanket earth in silken grace,
A serene glow, the world's embrace.
With every drift, a hush descends,
As peace envelops, time suspends.

From branches bare to rooftops high,
The shimmer weaves an artful tie.
In winter's arms, so calm, so light,
We find our joy in shimmering white.

And in the hush, our worries fade,
In quiet moments, memories made.
With heart aglow, we walk anew,
In this celestial view so true.

Radiance Wrapped in Winter's Embrace

The sun dips low, a golden line,
In winter's grip, the world does shine.
Each flake of snow, a radiant hue,
Wrapped in warmth, a lovely view.

The trees stand tall, their branches bare,
Adorned in crystals, everywhere.
As twilight paints the falling light,
With every breath, the air feels right.

In gentle hush, the evening glows,
While laughter echoes, warmth it sows.
Around the fire, stories embraced,
In winter's hold, our hearts are graced.

The beauty lies in moments shared,
In frosty nights, when love is bared.
And wrapped in dreams, we find our place,
In radiance wrapped in winter's embrace.

Starry Whispers in the Winter's Heart

In the stillness, stars align,
Softly glowing, they entwine.
Whispers echo through the dark,
As winter calls, a gentle spark.

Snowflakes dance on cold, crisp breeze,
Melodies weave through frozen trees.
Hearts entwined, they share the night,
Underneath that celestial light.

Silent wishes on the air,
Hope resides, free from despair.
In the quiet, dreams take flight,
In the starry whispers bright.

Embers glowing with the snow,
Warmth in hands, a tender glow.
In winter's heart, love will remain,
Through snow and silence, joy sustain.

Together beneath the vast expanse,
Filled with wonder, hearts in dance.
Starry whispers in the night,
Guide us home with pure delight.

Glowing Dreams on a Snow-Covered Night

Blankets white on a silent street,
Each step whispers soft and sweet.
Moonbeams glisten on the ground,
In this magic, beauty found.

Dreams arise in the frosty air,
Woven gently, beyond compare.
Stars like gems in a navy sea,
Illuminate what dreams can be.

Echoes of laughter fill the night,
Chasing shadows, pure delight.
Footprints trace a tale of yore,
In this wonder, we explore.

Crisp and clear, the world awakes,
Every heartbeat, softly shakes.
Glowing dreams in winter's lace,
Wrap us in its warm embrace.

Through the silence, spirits soar,
With every heartbeat, we want more.
In snow-covered realms, dreams ignite,
Guiding us through the night.

Whispers of Winter's Gaze

In the hush of falling snow,
Winter's whispers start to flow.
Softly spoken, secrets shared,
In this season, hearts are bared.

Moonlight casts a silver sign,
Guiding souls with gentle lines.
In the frost, a warmth remains,
In every drop, love refrains.

Stars align like scattered dreams,
In the night, a glow redeems.
Echoes of laughter fill the space,
In every shadow, winter's grace.

Crystals twinkle on the trees,
Nature's art; a perfect freeze.
Whispers linger in the air,
In this magic, none can compare.

Through the chill, our spirits rise,
In the dark, we find our ties.
Whispers of winter's gaze so bright,
Igniting love in the night.

Moonlight on Frosted Fields

Moonlight dances on the snow,
Waves of silver, soft and slow.
Frosted fields, a mystic sight,
Underneath the shimm'ring light.

Every flake tells a story clear,
Silent moments, held so dear.
In the stillness, we will tread,
Dreams enshrined where paths are led.

Gentle whispers of the night,
Fill the air, a soothing light.
In every shimmer, hopes take flight,
As we wander through the night.

Stars like lanterns guide the way,
Through the frost, where shadows play.
In moonlit fields, we find our rest,
Wrapped in warmth, forever blessed.

Nature's lullaby, soft and sweet,
Underneath the winter's sheet.
Moonlight whispers, hearts at ease,
In this moment, we find peace.

Celestial Whispers Among Snowflakes

In the stillness of night,
Snowflakes drift and glide,
Whispers of stars above,
In silence, they abide.

Each flake, a tale untold,
Carried on the breeze,
Dancing through the cold,
A melody of ease.

Softly they blanket earth,
Cloaking all in white,
Mapping dreams of worth,
In the soft moonlight.

Glimmers on the branches,
Nature's art displayed,
As time softly prances,
In a world remade.

Celestial secrets found,
In the frozen air,
Magic all around,
A spell beyond compare.

A Dance of Moonlit Frost

Beneath the silver glow,
Frost paints the ground,
A dance of shadows flow,
As night spins round.

Each step a soft embrace,
The earth, crisp and clear,
Moonlight's gentle grace,
Whispers warm and near.

Crystalline and bright,
The world glimmers white,
A silent symphony,
Unfolds in the light.

The trees sway and bend,
In a graceful trance,
With the night they blend,
In a frosty dance.

Lost in this moment,
Time drifts like a dream,
In shadows and scent,
Life's eternal scheme.

Dreaming Under the Icy Veil

Under the frosty sky,
Dreams take their flight,
Wrapped in a blanket high,
Of shimmering light.

The stars softly twinkle,
Glimmers on the frost,
In silence, they sprinkle,
What was once lost.

Fields lie still and white,
Nature's quiet song,
In the hush of night,
Where hearts can belong.

Whispers of the past,
Echo through the trees,
In every breath cast,
Carried on the breeze.

Beneath the icy veil,
Hope resides anew,
In dreams that prevail,
Life's beauty shines through.

Shimmering Silence in Winter's Embrace

In winter's warm embrace,
Silence drapes the plains,
A crystalline lace,
Where peace gently reigns.

The moonlight softly glows,
On the snow below,
As time quietly flows,
In the tranquil glow.

Footsteps leave a mark,
On this canvas wide,
A journey from the dark,
With nature as guide.

Each breath, a frosted sigh,
In the chill of night,
Underneath the sky,
Everything feels right.

Wrapped in this stillness,
Heartbeats all around,
In shimmering softness,
Joy can here be found.

Dreamscapes in White Haze

In the veil of mist we tread,
Whispers of silence fill the air.
Shadows dance in dreams unsaid,
Serenity lingers everywhere.

Softly glowing, the world transforms,
Soft snowflakes drift on gentle breeze.
Each corner wrapped in nature's charms,
Winter's embrace puts hearts at ease.

Footprints fade as time stands still,
Every moment etched in ice.
Silent echoes, winter's will,
Dreams unfold, a paradise.

Beneath the hush, the world can breathe,
Frozen tales in crystal light.
In this haze, I find reprieve,
Lost in dreams, I take flight.

As the sun sets, shadows play,
Echoes of a soft goodbye.
In the night, we'll find our way,
Guided by the moonlit sky.

Moonlit Paths Through Winter's Caress

Beneath the friendly moon's bright glow,
Paths of silver twinkle and gleam.
In the stillness, quiet snow,
Guides us deeper into a dream.

Trees adorned in frosty lace,
Whisper tales of winter's night.
Each step taken, a slow embrace,
Wrapped in shadows, soft and light.

Crisp air carries scents of pine,
Nights that spark with boundless cheer.
In this world, the heart aligns,
Finding peace as all draws near.

Celestial paths beneath we tread,
Each heartbeat echoes, strong and true.
Where silence reigns, sweet thoughts are bred,
In winter's arms, I walk with you.

As dawn awakens dreams entwined,
From quiet night to morning's grace.
In moonlit love, we've truly mined,
Secrets whispered in winter's face.

The Glorious Hush of Winter Evenings

When twilight falls, a hush descends,
Blankets of white, a calming sight.
Evening whispers, where silence bends,
Nights wrapped in soft, pure delight.

Candles flicker, casting dreams,
Shadows dance in the pale light.
Hot cocoa warms, its rich dark streams,
Filling hearts with cozy might.

Outside, the world in quiet pause,
Each breath a cloud of sparkling frost.
Nature's canvas, without flaws,
Captures moments, never lost.

In the stillness, we find a spark,
Magic lingers in the air.
Wrapped together as it gets dark,
Time feels endless, a sweet affair.

As stars unfold in the deepening blue,
Winter evenings hold us tight.
In the warmth of love so true,
We embrace the glorious night.

Echoes of Light in the Snow

In winter's arms, the world awakes,
Echoes dance, a playful tune.
Each flake falls softly, nothing breaks,
Wrapping all in a crystal cocoon.

Footsteps crunch in the silver night,
Moments linger, soft and clear.
Every shadow finds its light,
In this wonder, stillness near.

The air is filled with sparkling dreams,
Stars above in their twinkling flight.
Nature whispers, the softest gleams,
Painting the world in shades of white.

Here, time slows, each second shines,
As the moon bathes the earth in glow.
Living poetry in gentle lines,
Breathless beauty cloaked in snow.

In the silence, stories flow,
Hearts entwine under starlit skies.
Echoes linger, softly aglow,
In the chill, love never dies.

Veils of Ice and Dreams Above

Veils of ice drape the silent trees,
Dreams above in the whispering breeze.
Each flake a shimmer, a secret to hold,
In the heart of winter, a story unfolds.

Darkness paints the world in quiet tones,
While shadows dance on the frozen stones.
Moonlight drapes its glow so white,
A tapestry woven in the still of the night.

Through frosted windows, the world appears,
A canvas of wonder that calms all fears.
In breathless moments, time seems to pause,
Captivating dreams fill the night with applause.

Whispers echo from the stars so bright,
Carrying tales through the endless night.
Each glimmer a promise, a spark of delight,
In veils of ice, our dreams take flight.

Underneath the wide and twinkling sky,
Hope takes root as the night passes by.
In the blanket of winter, we find our way,
Veils of ice wrap our dreams till the day.

The Charmed Elegance of a Winter Night

In the stillness of the moonlit glow,
The charm of winter begins to flow.
Snowflakes drift like feathers so light,
Adorning the world in elegant white.

Whispers of frost in the chilly air,
A dance of shadows, a moment rare.
Each breath we take, a soft cloud rise,
In the elegance found beneath the skies.

Flickering candles, their warm embrace,
Illuminating smiles on every face.
The night wraps us in its tender guise,
As we watch the stars spark and surprise.

Silently gleaming, the earth is adorned,
With every heartbeat, our spirits warmed.
In the magic of winter, our hearts unite,
Celebrating the charm of this winter night.

Joyful laughter echoes in the cold,
Stories shared and memories told.
The elegance whispers in every sight,
As we embrace the beauty so bright.

Celestial Whispers Amidst Frozen Winds

Celestial whispers through the frozen trees,
A melody carried by the crisp, cold breeze.
Stars twirl above with a shimmering light,
Guiding our dreams through the veil of night.

In the still of the dark, the world feels alive,
With secrets and stories each star will contrive.
Frozen winds sing of places afar,
As we gaze in wonder at the night's bright star.

Pale moonlight cascades over fields of white,
Casting shadows and glimmers, enchanting the night.
Each breath we take is a wish on the soar,
In the arms of the cosmos, we long for more.

Wanderers' hearts find solace and peace,
In the celestial dance, our worries cease.
With frozen winds, our spirits entwined,
We dream of the stars and all that we find.

Amidst the chill, warmth is yet found,
In the whispers of heaven that softly surround.
Night unfolds gently with each passing hour,
Binding us close in winter's sweet power.

Frosted Stars Adrift in Night's Embrace

Frosted stars twinkle in the crisp night air,
Adrift on waves of a cosmic affair.
Each spark a promise, a tale to unveil,
In night's gentle embrace, we set sail.

The moon casts shadows on the glistening ground,
Silent whispers echo, a profound sound.
With every heartbeat, the universe sways,
In the beauty of the night, our spirits blaze.

Glistening branches, cloaked in pure frost,
Time stands still, we count not the cost.
In the stillness, our worries take flight,
As dreams take form in the depths of the night.

Beneath the vast dome, we find solace here,
With every frosted star, we draw near.
In the embrace of the night, we ignite,
The warmth of our hearts in the shimmering light.

Frosted dreams weave through the dark expanse,
In the dance of the cosmos, we take our chance.
Together we linger, in twilight we trace,
The frosted stars adrift in night's embrace.

A Serenade of Snowflakes

Softly they fall from the sky,
Whirling and dancing, oh so light.
Each one unique as a sigh,
Creating a blanket, pure and white.

Glistening under the pale moon,
They cradle the earth in their embrace.
A gentle and tranquil tune,
Nature's lullaby, time slows its pace.

Children laugh, their faces aglow,
Building snowmen, chasing delight.
With each flake, magic will grow,
As shadows stretch, fading from sight.

Whispers of winter draw near,
In frozen stillness, secrets unfold.
Hearts wrapped warm from the chill we fear,
Together we cherish the beauty of old.

As dawn breaks, hues of gold,
The snowflakes shimmer, farewell to night.
In this moment, life's stories told,
A serenade of snowflakes takes flight.

Luminous Frost Beneath a Velvet Canopy

In the hush of the frozen air,
A tapestry glows under the stars.
Frosted branches, a sight so rare,
Whisper dreams from lands afar.

Shimmering crystals, they catch the light,
A dance of glory, nature's delight.
Each breath exhaled, a cloud takes flight,
Under this canopy, all feels right.

Embraced by the night's gentle hold,
The world transformed, so pure, so bright.
Soft shadows painted in silver and gold,
As heartbeats echo, banishing fright.

Time stands still in the moon's warm glow,
With whispers of magic in the air.
Luminous frost, delighting the soul,
Wrapping us close in winter's fair.

Awakened dreams beneath the tree,
In a realm where silence sings.
Nature's beauty, serene and free,
Beneath this weave of frosted wings.

Twinkling Tranquility in Frozen Silence

Beneath the stars, a soft hush lies,
Where frost kisses earth, a gentle sigh.
The world wrapped in white, under night skies,
Twinkling tranquility, as moments pass by.

Each flake drifts down with elegance rare,
Whispers of peace float on the air.
Trees adorned, a tranquil affair,
In this frozen silence, burdens we bear.

Footsteps crunch in the powdery snow,
Echoes of laughter, pure joy in tow.
Moonlight dances, casting a glow,
In the heart of winter, magic will grow.

Frost retreats as dawn comes near,
Painting the landscape with colors so bright.
A canvas of white, a dreamer's sphere,
Crafted in silence, kissed by the light.

In frozen moments, we find our place,
Lost in the beauty that nature provides.
Twinkling tranquility, a warm embrace,
Winter's soft whispers in tranquil rides.

Enchanted Whispers of the Cold

Amidst the chill of an evening's grace,
Enchanted whispers echo and play.
The world transformed, a still embrace,
As frosted branches hold night at bay.

Snowflakes flutter, each one a thought,
Caught in the dance of the winter's breath.
Echoes of stories that time forgot,
Linger softly in the silence of death.

Under the spell of the moonlit glow,
Nature hums a soft lullaby.
With every breath, the cold winds blow,
Cradling the earth as night drifts by.

A symphony swells in the heart of freeze,
The world rests easy on winter's lap.
Drifting farther, we move with ease,
In the comfort of cold's gentle map.

Beneath the stars that shimmer and shine,
Mysteries unfold as shadows part.
Enchanted whispers, delicately divine,
Kiss the fabric of the dreaming heart.

Winter's Glimmering Poetry Unfolds

Snowflakes dance upon the breeze,
Their whispers tell of quiet ease.
Each crystal forms a tale so bright,
In wintry chill, a spark of light.

Branches bow beneath the weight,
Nature's art as dreams await.
A blanket soft, pure white and still,
Winter's grace atop the hill.

Fires crackle, warmth inside,
As frost encases all outside.
Laughter echoes, spirits high,
In this season, hearts can fly.

Footprints trace a secret path,
In the stillness, calm and math.
Stars above begin to gleam,
In winter's hush, we find our dream.

The world transformed in icy glow,
A wondrous place, serene and slow.
Nature's canvas, vast and wide,
Winter's magic, our hearts glide.

Dreamy Trails on a Midnight Canvas

Stars like diamonds scatter bright,
In the cloak of velvet night.
Whispers travel on the breeze,
Through the trees, in gentle tease.

Moonlight spills on paths so fair,
Illuminating dreams laid bare.
Each step echoes in soft tones,
Guiding hearts through twilight zones.

Shadows dance beneath the glow,
Secrets murmur, tales unfold.
Every trail a story new,
In midnight's charm, our spirits grew.

Pondering under the darkened sky,
Wonders beckon, we'll soar high.
On this canvas, vast and deep,
Dreams awaken, softly creep.

Nature whispers, secrets shared,
In the night, we are unpaired.
Endless skies invite our souls,
On this journey, the heart unrolls.

Seraphic White Under Celestial Beams

Angelic snowflakes swirl and glide,
Beneath the stars that brightly guide.
A tranquil hush, a world reborn,
In soft embrace of winter's morn.

Heaven's light on frosted ground,
Whispers of love in silence found.
In every flake, a prayer takes flight,
As day breaks softly into night.

Crystal visions, pure and fair,
In the air, a peace laid bare.
Hearts entwined in soft refrain,
In the dance of snow, we remain.

A sacred glow, the trees stand tall,
Underneath this ethereal call.
Threads of silver interlace,
Seraphic warmth fills this space.

Embracing the wonder, lost in time,
Every moment, a soft rhyme.
In winter's arms, we find release,
Beneath the beams, our souls find peace.

Glacial Elegance in the Night Air

Whispers of frost on silent ground,
In glacial beauty, peace is found.
Moonlit paths invite the gaze,
Twinkling stories in the haze.

Each breath a cloud in crisp expanse,
Nature's rhythm, a wondrous dance.
Starlit dreams weave through the dark,
In icy quiet, we embark.

Branches shimmer, draped in white,
A vision born from winter's might.
Elegance shines in the night air,
A seamless blend of magic rare.

Whirlwinds swirl, enchanting sight,
Painting landscapes, pure delight.
Footprints echo tales long told,
In glacial air, our hearts uphold.

As dawn approaches, colors bloom,
The world awakens from its gloom.
In winter's grasp, we find our way,
In night's embrace, forever stay.

Sparkling Dreams in Midnight White

In the still of night, stars shine bright,
Whispers of dreams take sudden flight.
Ethereal glow fills the air,
Every heartbeat, a silent prayer.

Moonlight dances on silver streams,
Casting shadows on hidden dreams.
Each flicker tells a tale anew,
Painting visions in shades of blue.

Clouds drift softly, secrets unfold,
Wrapped in wonder, a story told.
Starlit wishes weave and twine,
In the realm where hearts align.

Night unfolds with a gentle gleam,
Cradling thoughts like a waking dream.
Each moment filled with endless grace,
As time begins to slow its pace.

In this hush, let feelings soar,
Embracing all that lies in store.
Sparkling dreams, forever bright,
In the magic of midnight light.

Celestial Flakes in a Silent Night

Glistening flakes cascade from above,
Whispering secrets, the night we love.
Each one a promise, soft and white,
In this world of magical delight.

Blankets of snow cover the ground,
Silence lingers, it's peace profound.
Footprints of dreams traced in the frost,
In this serene beauty, we are lost.

Stars peek out from the velvet dome,
Guiding wanderers far from home.
Hearts entwined in the quiet glow,
As celestial flakes begin to flow.

With every drift, we find our way,
In the stillness, where minds can play.
The night is painted in soft embrace,
As dreams awaken in time and space.

Beneath the sky, we stand aligned,
In wonder, all worries unconfined.
Celestial flakes, a gentle flight,
In the stillness of this silent night.

Glistening Echoes of the Night Sky

In the deep blue, echoes call,
Stars reflecting, we rise and fall.
The night speaks soft, in whispers low,
A symphony of light, a cosmic show.

Galaxies spin in a dance divine,
Each twinkle woven in the fabric of time.
Glistening threads, like dreams unfurled,
A tapestry bright, this starlit world.

Voices of night carry on the breeze,
Hints of magic that put hearts at ease.
In the vastness, we find our place,
Embracing shadows with gentle grace.

With every glance towards the vast sky,
We gather hope as the moments fly.
Echoes of laughter, stories shared,
In the dark, love is always declared.

As constellations guide our way,
In this wonder, we long to stay.
Glistening echoes dance and play,
In the silence, we find our sway.

Crystal Dreams Under a Shimmering Veil

Beneath a sky of diamond hues,
We wander paths where magic brews.
Crystal dreams unfold at night,
Wrapped in whispers of pure delight.

Gentle starlight drapes the land,
A shimmering gift, a tender hand.
Each step taken on silken air,
In this realm, we shed our care.

The veil of night, a sacred space,
Where time stands still, a warm embrace.
Echoes of hopes rise up to soar,
Leading us to an open door.

In the glow of dreams, we find our way,
Underneath the twilight's sway.
Crystals glimmer, hearts unfold,
As love experiences manifold.

Softly we dance on the edge of night,
Wrapped in visions, so pure, so bright.
Crystal dreams under stars prevail,
In the wonder of a shimmering veil.

Nightfall's Embrace Beneath the Snow

Whispers of night, softly descend,
Under the blanket where darkness blends.
Stars twinkle keen, a silent spark,
Guiding the world through shadows dark.

Snowflakes dance in a gentle swirl,
Crystals of light in a quiet world.
Each flake a story, a whisper of dreams,
Caught in the web of moonlit beams.

Branches bow low, heavy with white,
Nature's adornment in stillness bright.
Footsteps muffled on soft, cold ground,
A chorus of silence, a peaceful sound.

Nightfall's embrace, a tranquil sigh,
Under the gaze of the starlit sky.
Beneath the snow, the earth finds rest,
In winter's arms, we are truly blessed.

The Quiet Waltz of Frost and Stars

In the velvet hush where night does creep,
Frost paints the window, secrets to keep.
Stars glimmer softly, a waltz of light,
Moving in rhythm with whispers of night.

The moon casts shadows that dance and play,
Leading the dreams that wander away.
Each breath of air is crisp and clear,
A moment to cherish, a time to revere.

Snowflakes glisten like diamonds aglow,
In the quiet waltz, they drift and flow.
Nature's heartbeat, a calm serenade,
In this tranquil world where worries fade.

Stars twinkle down in the frosty air,
A celestial ballet, beyond compare.
Each sparkle a promise, a dream to behold,
In the quiet waltz, our hearts unfold.

Snow Serenades Under the Moon

Serenades rise in the chill of night,
Snowflakes whisper, their dance takes flight.
Moonlight embraces the world below,
Casting a spell in the soft, white glow.

Trees wear pearls like a bride's delight,
Sparkling softly in the still of night.
Songs of the forest drift through the trees,
Carried by winds that hum with ease.

In this wonderland, the heart sings true,
Each note a promise, each flake anew.
Under the moon's watchful, silver eye,
Snow serenades tell the world goodbye.

Capturing moments, ephemeral grace,
Nature's own rhythm, an endless embrace.
Beneath the calm, our spirits ignite,
In snow serenades, our souls take flight.

Silhouettes of Joy in a White Canvas

On winter's canvas, all is aglow,
Silhouettes of joy in the soft, fresh snow.
Laughter and light in the frosty air,
Each moment treasured, a memory rare.

Children's footprints map out their play,
Creating a story in the crisp, bright day.
Snowmen stand guard with their carrot noses,
Chasing the chill where happiness floses.

Hot cocoa waits by the fireside bright,
Warming our hearts on a cold, starry night.
Wrapped in blankets, we share our dreams,
In this white canvas, life's beauty gleams.

Hope dances lightly on each falling flake,
Carrying wishes that winter can make.
Silhouettes of joy, forever alive,
Painting our hearts with the bliss to thrive.

Illuminated Silence of the Frosted Realm

In the frosted night so still,
Shimmers dance on trees so high,
Whispers wrap the world in chill,
Underneath the pale moon's eye.

Crystals twinkle, softly gleam,
Branches drape in icy lace,
Frozen rivers, silent stream,
Nature's breath in a quiet space.

Footsteps echo, muffled sound,
Snowflakes gently touch the ground,
Each breath rises, trembles free,
In this realm, just you and me.

Stars above, a diamond glow,
Covering the earth in light,
Time stands still as night winds blow,
Wrapped in peace, a pure delight.

Here we find our whispered dreams,
Wrapped in warmth of frosted night,
Boundless skies and silver beams,
Carried forth in joy's sweet flight.

A Dance of Light in the Snow's Embrace

Underneath the winter's quilt,
Glowing softly, shadows play,
In the hush where silence built,
Magic weaves, it lights the way.

Figures twirl with graceful flair,
Snowflakes spin, a swirling trance,
Every breath a frozen prayer,
In this cold, a joyful dance.

Glistening paths that intertwine,
Footprints whisper stories past,
In this realm where hearts align,
Moments held within the vast.

Fires crackle, warmth takes hold,
Laughter echoes through the night,
Hand in hand, our dreams unfold,
In the glow of soft moonlight.

As the dawn begins to rise,
Colors burst with sweet surprise,
But the magic of the night,
Lives within our hearts so bright.

Echoing Silence Amidst Silver Lumens

In the hush of silver beams,
Lights reflect on icy plains,
Lost within our tangled dreams,
A world shimmers, breaks the chains.

Stillness reigns where shadows lie,
Nature's pulse, a gentle thrum,
Listen close, hear whispers sigh,
In the night, the melodies hum.

Every flake a story spun,
Gold and silver intertwine,
Underneath the endless sun,
Moments caught in frozen time.

Dancing lights from stars above,
Kites of lumens, bright and bold,
Cocooned in a tapestry of love,
A sight more precious than gold.

Amidst the echoing silence here,
Hearts will beat with tender grace,
Lost in wonder, we draw near,
In this calm, we've found our place.

Whimsical Drift of Crystal Night

Snowflakes waltz on winter's breeze,
Whispers twirling through the air,
Dancing softly with such ease,
Twirling dreams without a care.

Moonlit paths where shadows sway,
Crystal frost on tranquil ground,
In the hush where night holds sway,
Nature's beauty, pure and profound.

Glistening wonders, drift and play,
Pillowed roofs and glittered trees,
Silent songs that softly lay,
In the wonders of the freeze.

Weaving tales of yore and new,
In this realm of joy and peace,
Every twinkling star renews,
Hope that never will cease.

As dawn's light begins to break,
With the sun, our dreams take flight,
In the heart, the memories wake,
From the whimsical drift of night.

Midnight Glimmers on White Whispers

In the silent night sky, stars gleam bright,
Whispers of winter dance in soft light.
Frosted branches sway with a gentle sigh,
Dreams take flight, as shadows pass by.

Moonbeams trace paths on a blanket of white,
Echoes of laughter float, pure delight.
Beneath the stillness, secrets unfold,
Stories of ages, in silence retold.

Each glimmer a wish, a promise of peace,
In the heart of the night, all troubles cease.
A canvas of calm where the wild things roam,
Midnight's embrace feels just like home.

Time drifts slowly in this frozen scene,
Dreams weave softly, a silvery sheen.
Nature holds breath; the world seems to pause,
Under the magic, we find our cause.

In twilight's hush, hearts find their grace,
Glimmers of hope in this sacred space.
As white whispers echo, the night extends,
A tapestry woven with love that transcends.

The Quiet Sparkle of Winter's Breath

Silent flakes fall, like whispers so fair,
Cloaking the earth in a blanket of care.
Each crystal shines with a delicate glow,
In winter's embrace, the world moves slow.

Pine trees adorned with nature's own art,
Frost-kissed branches, a wintery heart.
Footsteps crunch softly on pathways of white,
Under the moon's watch, everything feels right.

The stillness surrounds, a breath held in time,
Hushed rhythms echo, a gentle rhyme.
Stars twinkle above, a celestial dome,
In the quiet sparkle, we're never alone.

Laughter rings out as snowflakes collide,
Around every corner, a wintery ride.
With each fleeting moment, our worries take flight,
We dance in the glow of the soft winter night.

In the hush of the season, hearts start to thaw,
The quiet of winter reveals nature's law.
With every deep breath, we gather our might,
In the sparkle of snow, our spirits take flight.

Moonlit Reveries Adrift in Snow

Beneath the silver haze, shadows tease,
In the arms of the night, the cold winds freeze.
Dreams drift softly on the crisp, white ground,
Moonlit whispers in silence abound.

Branches reach out, dipped in soft glow,
A tapestry woven where moments flow.
Gentle giggles break through the serene,
A world transformed by the sights unseen.

Footsteps echo on the fresh fallen snow,
In each little crunch, the heart feels the glow.
Carried by starlight, hopes rise and fall,
In the vastness of winter, we hear winter's call.

Clouds drift lazily, curtains of night,
Cradling dreams until dawn's early light.
With each silver beam, our spirits unchain,
In the moonlit reveries, peace flows like rain.

Softly we wander through pathways of white,
Kissed by the magic of this winter night.
With open hearts, we embrace the unknown,
In moonlit dreams, we find our way home.

Celestial Tapestry on Winter's Canvas

Stars stitch the sky in a delicate thread,
While the world sleeps wrapped in a blanket of dread.
Snowflakes twirl gently, a dance of their own,
Whispering tales of the cold and alone.

Each breath a cloud in the stillness profound,
Nature hums softly, a comforting sound.
In this frozen wonder, hearts learn to feel,
Beneath cosmic blankets, the world starts to heal.

Every flake unique, a masterpiece spun,
In winter's embrace, we are one with the sun.
Timeless and tranquil, the night holds its grace,
A celestial canvas, painted with space.

Frosted horizons stretch far and wide,
Where dreams scatter freely, and fears can reside.
Each glimmer a beacon, a light in the dark,
In the tapestry of winter, we leave our mark.

Wrapped in the stillness, we find our way,
Through the magic of winter, we cherish the day.
In every soft whisper, in every moonbeam,
We weave our own stories, we dance and we dream.

Ethereal Glow in the Chilling Breeze

A whisper soft in twilight's hold,
A dance of light, both faint and bold.
The air, it shimmers, crisp and clear,
Inviting warmth, drawing us near.

Among the shadows, spirits wane,
With every breath, we feel the strain.
Yet hope ignites in gentle hues,
As stars awaken, sharing clues.

Beneath the moon, the world ignites,
In fragile beams, the heart delights.
Each moment sways in the night's embrace,
A fleeting glimpse of timeless grace.

Through frosty air, the echoes call,
Of whispered dreams that never fall.
In every chill, a warmth resides,
A soothing balm where love abides.

Ethereal glow, we stand enthralled,
In nature's grasp, we've gently stalled.
With open arms, we take a breath,
In silent nights, we cheat the death.

Luminous Frost Among the Timber

In silent woods where silence reigns,
The frost unfolds its crystal chains.
Each branch adorned in glistening light,
A shimmering cloak that veils the night.

Through frozen glades, a gentle dance,
Of chilly winds that swirl and prance.
The timber whispers tales of old,
In frosty breath, their mysteries told.

Moonlit paths weave through the trees,
As shadows play with winter's breeze.
With every step, the earth ignites,
In echoes soft, the woods invite.

The crystalline air, so sweetly stirs,
Awakens dreams, a world of hers.
Among the timber, still and proud,
Transformation hidden under shroud.

Luminous frost, a scene divine,
Where whispered moments intertwine.
Embracing silence, hearts we mend,
In nature's arms, we find our friend.

Nightfall's Enchantment on Silent Streets

As night descends on slumbered towns,
With lanterns casting gentle crowns.
The quiet streets, a mystic dance,
Where shadows weave a timeless trance.

Cobblestones, with stories lined,
In whispers soft, the past entwined.
Each corner turned, a secret smiles,
Beneath the stars, a million miles.

The moonbeams play on windows wide,
Reflecting dreams that do not hide.
In every echo, hearts align,
With hope and warmth, the world divine.

A sudden breeze brings tales anew,
Of laughter shared, of love so true.
With every footfall, magic grows,
On silent streets, where mystery flows.

Nightfall's charm, an endless muse,
In every heartbeat, rhythms fuse.
As dawn approaches, shadows fade,
In night's embrace, we've softly stayed.

Glacial Echoes of Distant Stars

In skies where dreams and galaxies meet,
Distant stars weave tales so sweet.
A glacial breath upon the night,
In sparkling hues, they share their light.

Across the void, the whispers soar,
Of ages past, of cosmic lore.
In every twinkle, stories blend,
A canvas vast where worlds ascend.

Frozen depths, reflections bright,
Each pinprick glows with ancient light.
Through endless space, the echoes sing,
Of time's embrace and wondrous things.

In silence deep, a truth appears,
That darkness holds a wealth of years.
Yet in that chill, our hearts ignite,
With every pulse, we share the night.

Glacial echoes, soft and clear,
A harmony that draws us near.
In cosmic dance, our spirits rise,
Embracing all beneath the skies.

The Soft Whistle of Chilling Dreams

In the quiet shadows of the night,
Whispers of frost take gentle flight.
Chilling dreams weave through the air,
Lacing the world with tender care.

Moonlight spills on silver trees,
Dancing softly with the breeze.
Each sighing branch tells a tale,
Of winter's breath, serene and pale.

Stars blink softly in the deep,
Cradling secrets that they keep.
Through the dark, a stillness reigns,
Echoes of joy amidst the pains.

In slumber's grip, all hearts align,
Finding solace, pure and divine.
As dreams take flight on chilling wings,
Every moment anew, it brings.

So let the soft whispers unfold,
In chilling dreams, our stories told.
Wrapped in warmth, we find our way,
Through the night to a brighter day.

Radiant Trails in the Silent Snow

Beneath the blanket, white and pure,
Silent whispers of nature's allure.
Footprints lead where dreams may roam,
In the snow, we find our home.

The world transformed beneath our feet,
Radiant trails, a wondrous treat.
Every step, a story spun,
In crisp dawn light, we greet the sun.

Soft flakes dance with a playful grace,
Carving joy in every space.
Life's moments captured in the chill,
Radiant hearts, forever will.

Pine trees sway in gentle cheer,
Nature's music, sweet and clear.
In the stillness, hope will grow,
With each breath, the love we sow.

As twilight paints the sky aglow,
Radiant trails weave through the snow.
In every flurry, a chance to play,
Embracing magic, come what may.

Glittering Fantasies Under a Cold Sky

Underneath the vast expanse,
Sparkling dreams begin to dance.
Cold winds whisper tales unknown,
In the night, our seeds are sown.

Glittering fantasies twinkle bright,
Guiding us through the endless night.
Each star a wish waiting to bloom,
Shining fervor through the gloom.

With every breath, the chill ignites,
A symphony of silent nights.
Embracing shadows, we take flight,
In a dreamscape bathed in light.

Upon the frost, we stake our claim,
In this world, we feel no shame.
Hand in hand, our spirits soar,
Through glittering dreams, forevermore.

So let us wander, lost in time,
Under the cold sky, we rhyme.
In every heartbeat, adventure calls,
As glittering fantasies fill our halls.

Opalescent Dreams Amidst the Chill

In the embrace of winter's night,
Opalescent dreams take to flight.
Softly glowing, whispers of peace,
In every heartbeat, troubles cease.

The air is crisp, a gentle sigh,
As twilight paints the starlit sky.
Every moment, rich and deep,
In the silence, our secrets keep.

Shimmers dance on frosted ground,
Where hidden magic can be found.
We'll trace our dreams in silver light,
As shadows wane and spirits bright.

Held within this twilight's grace,
Opalescent dreams we trace.
With open hearts, we softly yield,
To the truths our souls have sealed.

In this chill, we find our spark,
Illuminating the deepest dark.
Embracing every fleeting thrill,
In opalescent dreams, we spill.

Whispering Hearts Beneath Frozen Dreams

In the silence, shadows play,
Whispers dance on frosty air.
Hearts entwined in night's embrace,
Dreams awaken, bright and fair.

Snowflakes twirl, a soft parade,
With each gust, the secrets flow.
Beneath the stars, promises fade,
As the world paints winter's glow.

Time stands still in these cold hours,
Memories wrapped in freezing light.
Hope unfurls like blossomed flowers,
In the stillness of the night.

We breathe in the crisp delight,
Sharing warmth where chill resides.
Underneath the moon's soft light,
Whispering hearts, where love abides.

Frosted dreams and tender sighs,
In this moment, we are one.
In the canvas of the skies,
Our frozen hearts have just begun.

Frost-Kissed Serenade of the Night

Beneath a quilt of shimmering white,
The world rests silent, deep in dreams.
Frost-kissed whispers, pure delight,
Echo softly, like laughter streams.

The moonlight paints the icy ground,
Stars twinkle with a gentle grace.
Nature's voice, a soothing sound,
In this moment, time's embrace.

Chill winds weave through pine and oak,
A serenade wrapped in the cold.
Each breeze a tale, softly spoke,
Of winter nights, both pure and bold.

In shadows deep, the world is still,
Every breath a piece of art.
The beauty here, it's hard to fill,
With warmth that blooms within the heart.

So let us dance beneath the stars,
In this frosty serenade's light.
With each note, we travel far,
Through the endless winter night.

A Starlit Blanket on the Earth

Silent night, the heavens gleam,
A starlit blanket on the earth.
Whispers float, a gentle dream,
In this space, we find our worth.

Softly wrapped in silver's glow,
Each twinkle tells a story bright.
Beneath the sky, our spirits flow,
Basking in the tranquil light.

Footprints hidden in the snow,
Mark the paths we've wandered long.
In the stillness, feelings grow,
Melodies of our shared song.

Hearts entwined beneath the sky,
A dance of warmth in chill's embrace.
In every breath, a whispered sigh,
The universe, our sacred space.

For in this night, all fears release,
And love ignites like starlit fire.
With every moment, find our peace,
Bathed in dreams, we rise, aspire.

Radiance in the Silence of Snow

In the quiet, snowflakes fall,
A radiant hush blankets the ground.
Whispers echo, soft and small,
In winter's arms, where love is found.

Frozen branches, jeweled sights,
The world transformed, pure and bright.
Silhouettes dance in pale moonlight,
Carrying wishes into the night.

Every flake a tale to tell,
Of moments frozen, never lost.
In this beauty, all is well,
Embracing warmth despite the frost.

We gather close, hearts beating near,
Wrapped in memories, soft and sweet.
In the silence, love is clear,
A bond that time can't erase or beat.

So let us cherish this embrace,
In the radiance of the snow.
Amongst the stillness, we find grace,
As winter's magic starts to show.

Radiant Silhouettes in Frosted Glow

In the hush of winter's embrace,
Shadows dance with gentle grace.
Frosty whispers lift the veil,
As twilight sings a frosted tale.

Trees adorned with sparkling light,
Glisten softly in the night.
Each branch a work of art displayed,
In nature's chill, the colors swayed.

Moonlight bathes the world in dreams,
Turning silence into gleams.
In the stillness hearts ignite,
Radiant silhouettes take flight.

Stars above, a canvas bright,
Guiding all with silver light.
A symphony of night unfurls,
In this magic, time whirls.

Wrapped in beauty, soft and slow,
We find warmth in the frosted glow.
Hand in hand, we'll wander free,
In this wonder, you and me.

Celestial Harmony in Frozen Time

In the arms of winter's chill,
The world rests, time stands still.
Whispers of the cosmos play,
In quietude, night meets day.

Stars align in perfect arc,
Illuminating every dark.
Frozen air, a crystal song,
Notes that echo, pure and strong.

With each flake, a tale is spun,
Of distant realms and lost sun.
Harmony in icy breath,
Fleeting echoes dance with death.

Veils of snow enshroud the land,
Nature's touch, a gentle hand.
In this stillness, hearts entwine,
Celestial treasures, yours and mine.

Time slips softly through the night,
Embraced by frost, adorned with light.
Together we will dream anew,
In frozen time, just me and you.

Serendipity in a Blanket of Snow

Beneath the hush of falling snow,
Life awakens, sweet and slow.
Whispers call from lands unknown,
In the silence, seeds are sown.

As we wander through the white,
Footprints trace our joyful flight.
Laughter dances in the air,
Fortune shines, a bright affair.

Every flake, a gift divine,
Wrapping dreams in icy twine.
Miracles in every fold,
Stories waiting to be told.

With each moment, fate aligns,
In the snow, a love that shines.
Hearts entwined, we leap and chase,
Finding joy in every space.

The world transformed, a pure delight,
A serendipity ignites.
In this blanket, soft and deep,
We discover what dreams keep.

Frosted Glories Beneath the Celestial Dome

Underneath the starlit skies,
Frosted glories begin to rise.
Nature's palette, bold and bright,
Whispers secrets through the night.

Icicles gleam like silver swords,
Nature's magic, spoken words.
In the stillness, dreams unwind,
All our hopes, forever twined.

With every breath, the cold exhales,
Tales of love in frosty gales.
Beneath the dome where wonders gaze,
Life reveals its quiet praise.

Snowflakes twirl like dancers fair,
Painting beauty everywhere.
In this moment, hearts align,
Frosted glories, yours and mine.

In the night, our spirits rise,
Underneath celestial ties.
Holding tight, we feel the glow,
In this haven, love will grow.

Soft Glimmers in a Frozen Universe

In a quiet night sky, stars begin to sway,
Whispers of light dance, leading dreams away.
Glimmers of silver brush the frozen trees,
Each twinkling echo stirs the gentle breeze.

Snowflakes drift softly, wrapped in pure white,
Carpeting the ground, a spellbinding sight.
Their graceful descent, a serene ballet,
Painting the world in a magical way.

Deep in the silence, the cosmos unfold,
Stories of wonder, waiting to be told.
Galaxies shimmer, like diamonds afar,
In this frozen universe where dreams are stars.

Beneath the moon's glow, secrets intertwine,
Nature whispers gently, a lullaby divine.
Every soft glimmer, a spark in the night,
Illuminating hearts, igniting delight.

In the depth of winter, where magic is spun,
Hope and serenity rise with the sun.
Soft glimmers awaken, a promise anew,
In this frozen universe, dreams will come true.

The Frosted Poetry of the Night

Under the cloak of a velvet sky,
Whispers of frost in the chill nearby.
Moonlight paints verses on the still ground,
In this frosted landscape, our dreams are found.

Stars break the silence with stories untold,
Each sparkling fragment, a memory bold.
Wrapped in the stillness, we breathe in the air,
Frosted poetry lingers, a moment to share.

Across the white canvas, shadows emerge,
Dancing in harmony, a gentle surge.
Under the winter's breath, warm hearts align,
In the frost of the night, our spirits entwine.

Every soft flake that tumbles to rest,
Carries a tale of the nature blessed.
In the chill of the evening, dreams take flight,
Embracing the beauty, we savor the night.

With each quiet inch, the world comes alive,
In the frosted embrace, our hopes will thrive.
Let us bask in the magic, the night is our stage,
We craft our own poems, forever to page.

Shadows and Snowflakes in Harmony

When winter descends, shadows start to play,
Snowflakes are partners, in a dance they sway.
Gently they tumble, a soft, silent song,
In this frozen moment, we all belong.

Under the moonlight, the world takes a breath,
Whispers of stillness imply life and death.
Each flake that flutters carries a tune,
Adding to the lively serenade of the moon.

The branches wear crystals, a crown made of light,
Nature's own artistry, pure and bright.
As shadows stretch longer, they start to embrace,
The magic of winter, a mystical space.

With every step taken in silence we find,
Harmony plays on, divine and aligned.
Each snowflake a note in this wintry refrain,
Painting the night sky, tender and humane.

Together they shimmer, shadows and light,
His tender embrace makes the darkness so bright.
In the dance of the snowflakes, life's rhythm is true,
In harmony's cradle, we find something new.

Silver Threads on a Quiet Night

On a quiet night, threads of silver weave,
Stories of old, in the stars we believe.
Each twinkle a promise, a wish on the rise,
Illuminating darkness with ancient ties.

Beneath the clear sky, the whispers take flight,
Carrying secrets through the velvet night.
Silver threads sparkle, a delicate lace,
Embracing the shadows, bestowing their grace.

Frost-kissed horizons, a shimmering band,
Guide us through mysteries, hand in hand.
In the glow of the night, hearts learn to soar,
Wrapped in warm dreams, forever we explore.

With each gentle breath, the universe sighs,
Each moment a treasure, a gift that implies.
Every silver thread, an eternal embrace,
Weaving together the fabric of space.

Under the starlight, in silence, we find,
The beauty around us, forever entwined.
On this quiet night, with silver so bright,
We dance with our dreams, in the soft moonlight.

Frosty Reveries of the Midnight Sky

Beneath a blanket of stars so bright,
The world is hushed, wrapped in the night.
Silent whispers in the chilling breeze,
Frosty dreams dance among the trees.

Moonlight glimmers on the frozen ground,
A silver shimmer, a tranquil sound.
Snowflakes twirl in the shimmering air,
A fleeting moment, a gentle prayer.

Echoes of laughter fade into the dark,
While shadows flicker, a tranquil spark.
Each breath visible in the crisp, cold space,
Caught in the stillness, a fragile grace.

Stars like diamonds, scattered and rare,
Weaving stories in the midnight air.
Time stands still in this frosty embrace,
In winter's wonder, we find our place.

So let us linger under this sky,
Where frosty reveries never die.
In the arms of night, dreams come alive,
In this frost-kissed realm, we learn to thrive.

A Tapestry of Glistening Moments

Threads of silver in the morning light,
Each moment woven, pure and bright.
The world awakens with a gentle sigh,
As daylight breaks, the shadows fly.

Sparkling dewdrops on blades of grass,
Whisper secrets of moments that pass.
A tapestry stitched with time's embrace,
Capture fleeting joys, a sacred space.

Children's laughter, a sweet refrain,
Echoes of joy like a soft, warm rain.
In every heartbeat, a story unfolds,
A gallery of life, rich and bold.

Glistening raindrops on window panes,
Nature's brush paints the streets with lanes.
Colors alive in the afternoon glow,
Moments like jewels, forever aglow.

So let us cherish each radiant thread,
In this tapestry where dreams are spread.
Together we weave, in love's sweet delight,
A tapestry of glistening light.

Winter's Glittering Caprice

A frosty morn, a dance of white,
Nature's mirth, a pure delight.
Icicles hang like crystal dreams,
Winter's magic flows in streams.

Snowflakes swirl in a playful race,
Each one unique, a fleeting grace.
Laughter echoes through the powdery drifts,
In winter's heart, our spirit lifts.

A world transformed, so bright and clear,
Every step whispers, winter is here.
Tracks of footprints in a frosty trace,
Leading us on through this silver lace.

With every breath, the air is sweet,
Cold kisses on our cheeks, so neat.
We twirl and spin in this snowy glow,
In winter's caprice, our hearts will flow.

So let us revel in this splendid scene,
In a world of wonder, vibrant and keen.
Winter's glitter, a brief interlude,
Lingers in joy, in each moment imbued.

Chasing Shadows in Crystal Light

Beneath the glow of a sunlit sky,
We chase our shadows as time slips by.
Every flicker, a story to tell,
In crystal light, where dreams dwell.

Moments captured in a golden hue,
Nature dances, alive and true.
Each ray a whisper, each shadow a song,
In this bright realm, we belong.

Fields of flowers in a vibrant spree,
Chasing shadows, wild and free.
Every heartbeat matches the light,
Every sigh echoes in delight.

With every step, the world unfolds,
Stories written in colors bold.
Lost in laughter, we twirl and glide,
Chasing shadows, side by side.

As daylight wanes, the dusk unfolds,
Whispers of twilight, secrets told.
In this dance of light, we take our flight,
Chasing shadows into the night.

Frosty Stars in the Midnight Sky

Whispers of winter dance so bright,
Frosty stars twinkle in the night.
Each sparkle tells a story old,
Of dreams and secrets yet untold.

A chill hangs softly in the air,
While silent shadows wander there.
The moon looks down with gentle grace,
Kissing the world, a soft embrace.

Beneath the icy, shimmering glow,
Nature sleeps, wrapped in silent snow.
The cosmos breathes a tranquil sigh,
As frosty stars light up the sky.

In feathered blankets, soft and white,
The world transforms in pure delight.
Each night brings magic to awake,
In this serene, enchanted lake.

Drawing my heart into the realms,
Where winter's beauty wears the crowns.
In every glance, I find my muse,
In frosty stars, with joy, I choose.

The Glimmering Blanket of Night

A blanket woven of dark and light,
Cloaks the earth in the hush of night.
Stars peep through with sparkling eyes,
Glimmering dreams in the velvet skies.

Whispers of wind through trees so tall,
Echo the night's enchanting call.
Each rustle sings a soothing tune,
As silver beams from the watchful moon.

The world pauses, heartbeat slows,
While darkness gracefully bestows.
A tranquil layer, soft and deep,
Wraps the world in a gentle sleep.

In shadows where memories hide,
The glimmering night becomes our guide.
We wander through the veils of dreams,
In moonlit paths, where magic gleams.

Embraced by night's serene caress,
We find the peace in darkness' dress.
In the glimmering blanket of stars,
We discover who we truly are.

Chasing Shadows in Winter's Glow

In the frosty air, shadows play,
Chasing whispers of light away.
Winter's glow wraps the world anew,
Painting the landscape in silver hue.

Footsteps crunch on the icy ground,
In the stillness, no other sound.
Each shadow dances, fleeting and free,
A mystical waltz back to me.

The evening sky, a canvas bold,
Streaked with hues of rose and gold.
A fading light, as day takes flight,
Chasing shadows into the night.

In the hush of snowflakes, dreams unfold,
Tales of winter lovingly told.
With every breath, the chill we know,
Brings warmth inside, a steady glow.

Embracing magic, the dusk descends,
As shadows blend, and light transcends.
Chasing echoes of warmth and light,
In winter's glow, we find our flight.

Ethereal Light on a Crystal Carpet

Ethereal light graces all it sees,
Draped on crystal carpets, soft as breeze.
Glistening pathways, a wintry show,
Invite our hearts to wander slow.

The world transforms in the dawn's embrace,
Each twinkle whispers of nature's grace.
With every step, the crystals spark,
A symphony sings in the quiet dark.

Snowflakes twirl in the gentle air,
Glowing softly without a care.
Every flake a tale to share,
With whispers woven through the fair.

Illuminated dreams take flight,
In the soft and tranquil light.
Each moment captured, pure delight,
As we dance on this crystal night.

In the warmth of winter's bright charade,
The ethereal light stops fear and fade.
We find our joy on a crystal path,
Where beauty reigns in winter's bath.

The Frosty Murmurs of Celestial Harmonies

In the quiet night sky, stars whisper soft,
Crystalline melodies, drifting aloft.
Snowflakes dance lightly on a shimmering breeze,
Nature's sweet symphony, bringing hearts ease.

Moonlight unveils the secrets of the deep,
Curtains of silver that gently creep.
A chorus of echoes in the frosty air,
Enveloping the world with a tender care.

Beneath the vast cosmos, silence sings bright,
Each twinkling star shines with a cool light.
The murmurs of winter, a lullaby grand,
Caressing the earth with a delicate hand.

Night's gentle whispers inspire the soul,
Filling the heart with a sense of whole.
Embraced by the night, we find pure delight,
In the frosty murmurs of celestial light.

Silvery Crystals Beneath the Twilight Glow

Beneath the twilight, a shimmer unfolds,
Silvery crystals, stories untold.
Glistening softly in the fading light,
Whispers of magic in the heart of the night.

A blanket of frost wraps the earth in dreams,
Reflecting the twilight's soft, gentle beams.
Every flake sparkling, a diamond in flight,
Painting the world in silver-white light.

The trees stand proud, adorned with a crown,
Each branch embracing winter's soft gown.
Nature's own canvas, bathed in blue hue,
Awakens a wonder, forever anew.

As shadows stretch long, the dusk takes its hold,
The beauty of winter, a sight to behold.
Silvery whispers, secrets they know,
Beneath the twilight, the crystals aglow.

Enchanted Nocturne of Snow and Light

In the silent night, a symphony plays,
Snowflakes twirl gently through the moon's rays.
Touching the ground like a lover's caress,
In shadows they dance, bringing happiness.

The world lies still, wrapped in a veil,
An enchanted nocturne, a soft fairy tale.
Each flake tells tales of joy and of peace,
A heartfelt reminder, our worries release.

Stars twinkle bright, their glimmers so rare,
Casting a glow on the frost-laden air.
While night sings along, with a melody sweet,
Snow and light waltz in a delicate beat.

The beauty of winter, ethereal sight,
Merging all dreams in the soft, velvet night.
Together they flourish, as one, as a whole,
An enchanted nocturne, soothing the soul.

Every moment a treasure, each breath a delight,
Wrapped in a wonder of snow and soft light.
This night holds the magic, the warmth of the kind,
As hearts beat together, forever entwined.

The Magic of Gentle Falling Flakes

Gentle falling flakes, like whispers from above,
Glimmering softly, they remind us of love.
A tapestry woven in purest of white,
Transforms the world into pure delight.

With every descent, the earth holds its breath,
As winter wraps all in the silence of death.
But life's in the stillness, a promise we find,
In the dance of each flake, intertwined, aligned.

The joy in the falling, the magic it brings,
Each snowy blanket, the joy that it sings.
A cascade of wonder, a shimmer of grace,
Falling from heaven, an endless embrace.

Nature's soft laughter, a lull in the air,
With each tiny flake, we shed all despair.
In moments of quiet, hearts begin to mend,
With magic of snowflakes, our worries suspend.

So let us rejoice in this wintery show,
The magic of falling, the beauty of snow.
Together we gather, as each flake alights,
Welcomed by wonder on soft, starlit nights.

Frosty Whispers Kissed by Starlight

In the stillness, snowflakes dance,
Silent whispers, a fleeting glance.
Stars above twinkle bright,
Guiding dreams in the crisp night.

Moonlight spills on frozen streams,
Crystals glisten like silver beams.
Nature wraps in a tender grace,
A moment caught in time and space.

Breathe in deep, the chill of air,
A world adorned with love and care.
Frosty patterns on windowpanes,
Whispered secrets in soft refrains.

Footprints trace a silent path,
In shimmering glow, we find our math.
Each step echoes with frosted cheer,
A night of magic, crystal clear.

As dawn approaches, shadows fade,
Yet memories in frost are laid.
Frosty whispers in the light,
Forever held in starlit night.

Marvels of Nightfall's Shimmering Canvas

Night descends, a velvet veil,
Stars emerge, a sparkling trail.
Moonlight paints the world anew,
Softened shadows blend in blue.

Whispers of the evening breeze,
Carry tales through the swaying trees.
Beauty unfolds with every sigh,
As darkness deepens in the sky.

Crickets sing their lullabies,
Underneath the vast, wide skies.
Each note a promise, sweet and clear,
In the hush, the world draws near.

Lanterns flicker, hope ignites,
Guiding hearts through starry nights.
Colors swirl in cosmic dance,
Nightfall weaves its wondrous trance.

Marvels crafted in twilight's hand,
A shimmering canvas, bold and grand.
Hold this moment, blissful, divine,
In the heart of night, we entwine.

The Enchantment of Frozen Light

In winter's grip, the world aglow,
A dreamlike realm where magic flows.
Frozen breath hangs in the air,
Whispers dance without a care.

Icicles glisten like crystal tears,
Reflecting hopes, dispelling fears.
Ethereal nights, a canvas white,
With every shimmer, pure delight.

Twilight drapes her silvery shawl,
Upon the earth, a sacred call.
Nature speaks in gentle tones,
In the quiet, we find our own.

Stars align in a cosmic play,
Guiding us on this frozen way.
Each flicker, a memory's trace,
In the stillness, we find our place.

Through snowy paths, our spirits soar,
An enchanted world forevermore.
Lost in the dance of frozen light,
Where dreams awaken in the night.

A Canvas of Dreams in Icy Tones

A canvas painted in icy hues,
Whispers of winter in the blues.
Each stroke, a memory wrapped in chill,
A symphony of stillness, artful thrill.

Frosted landscapes, serene and bright,
Glisten softly in the pale moonlight.
Echoes of laughter in the air,
Moments cherished, beyond compare.

Snowflakes fall like gentle grace,
Unique and fragile in their embrace.
Crisp and clear, the world awakes,
With every breath, the silence shakes.

In this realm of icy dreams,
Nature whispers in silver streams.
Holding secrets of ages past,
In the frosty air, our hearts are cast.

As dawn approaches, colors glow,
An artist's palette, a dazzling show.
In the canvas of dreams we find,
The purest magic of every kind.

Milton Keynes UK
Ingram Content Group UK Ltd.
UKHW010227111224
452348UK00011B/569